Wymondham and Attleborough

IN OLD PHOTOGRAPHS

Wymondham and Attleborough

IN OLD PHOTOGRAPHS

PHILIP YAXLEY

Alan Sutton Publishing Limited
Phoenix Mill · Far Thrupp · Stroud
Gloucestershire

First Published 1994

British Library Cataloguing in Publication Data.
A catalogue record for this book is available from
the British Library.

ISBN 0-7509-0749-5

Typeset in 9/10 Sabon.
Typesetting and origination by
Alan Sutton Publishing Limited.
Printed in Great Britain by
Hartnolls, Bodmin, Cornwall.

Contents

Wymondham's famous North Mill, once a landmark for miles around. In 1858 John Cann, a local entrepreneur, had this fine smock mill dismantled at Dilham and brought by the railway to Wymondham, where it was reassembled on a site off the Barnham Broom Road at Northfield. In 1900 the mill was one of three operating in the town, but in 1950 a terrible fire destroyed it (see page 112).

A huge crack in the great west tower of Wymondham Abbey Church in the late 1890s. The tower was built in the fifteenth century by the townspeople with the aid of Sir John Clifton. The crack was made good in a major restoration of the church between 1901 and 1905. Mrs Clara Willett, daughter of a former vicar, contributed £14,000 of the total cost of the restoration amounting to £20,249.

Introduction

Wymondham and Attleborough, where the martyred King Edmund is reputed to have resided for a year, were probably considerable settlements in Saxon times. However, it was after the Normans arrived that they became established market towns.

In 1107 William d'Albini founded Wymondham Priory, complete with parish church, and his son, also named William, built the castle at New Buckenham, which likewise became a market centre. From the twelfth to the fourteenth century at Attleborough, the Mortimers, another powerful family, were guiding affairs; it was Sir William de Mortimer who founded the Chapel of the Holy Cross, which forms the south transept of Attleborough Church, in the thirteenth century.

Wymondham's right to hold a Friday market was confirmed by King John in 1203, while Attleborough's Thursday market dates back to 1285. These markets served a neighbourhood which the agriculturalist Nathaniel Kent described much later in 1794 as 'equal to the finest land in the county'.

The advent of the railway in 1845 had an adverse effect on the local markets, as Norwich became much more accessible; but the markets have survived, though nowadays gaily coloured stalls cannot be seen in Church Street, Attleborough. Weekly auctions of livestock, and Attleborough's famous Michaelmas turkey sales, are now just history, but Wymondham still enjoys a fortnightly auction of furniture and the like.

With the arrival of the railway, industry encroached on what had been largely agricultural communities. In 1896 Gaymer's moved their cider operation to Attleborough to be near the railway, while at Wymondham trains transported flints and brushes from the town. Today, Wymondham has no brushmaking industry, but like Attleborough it is home to many small industrial units, and Lotus Cars Ltd is on the doorstep. Unlike fifty years ago, many workers now find employment in Norwich.

The past has not been without turbulent times. In 1549 the peasants under Wymondham's Robert Kett rebelled against injustices, including the enclosure of common land by harsh landlords. After initial success, the rebellion was crushed, and Kett, together with other leaders including his brother, William, was executed. Today, locals regard him as a hero.

In 1559 a huge fire ripped the heart out of Attleborough, while an even bigger blaze at Wymondham in 1615 saw 327 homes and several public buildings go up in smoke. In more recent times it has been man who has been the destroyer. Attleborough's historic College House and Wymondham's King's Head Inn are just two of many buildings which have been swept away in

Roger Pettit at work in the cooper's shop at Gaymer's cider factory in Attleborough, *c.* 1950. He joined the firm in 1921 and gave many years service. Pettit was a fine footballer with Attleborough Town FC.

'developments'. Though they have suffered the ravages of fire, albeit not on the same scale, towns like New Buckenham and Hingham remain largely unspoilt.

Attleborough and Wymondham have shared many experiences, notably in two world wars, but through the years they have competed in a friendly rivalry. In 1909 Wymondham folk were dismayed when the famous Whit Thursday sports were dropped and Attleborough staged the top meetings. However, in 1935 highly competitive 'old stagers' soccer matches saw Wymondham Crocks defeat Attleborough Veterans 4–2 and 4–1, but everyone was happy as all the proceeds from the games went to the Wymondham and Attleborough Nursing Association funds.

Occasions like these are now part of local folklore, and despite their seemingly ever-nearer proximity to Norwich, the towns have strived to maintain their identities. Be it turkey sales or woodturning, Attleborough and Wymondham are justly proud of their heritage and traditions.

Attleborough Scenes

The Griffin and the Angel inns in Church Street (once called Town Street) in 1908. Dating from the early sixteenth century, the Griffin was a posting inn of importance in the early nineteenth century when the Royal Mail coach stopped there on its Norwich to London run. The hostelry had survived a serious fire in 1762 when two houses and stables had been destroyed. The Angel opposite was once a popular hotel, but the building is now occupied by the Nationwide Building Society. The offices of Salter Simpson and Sons, auctioneers and estate agents, are shown next to the Griffin while the horse and cart are outside William Stebbings and Son, ironmongers and later cycle and motor engineers. They had been established in 1866 and served the town for generations.

St Mary's Church makes a wonderful winter scene in 1908. However, the photograph was taken on 24 April when almost five inches of snow fell! The church dates mostly from the fourteenth century, although the lower portions of the tower are Norman. It boasts a magnificent rood screen.

Church Street in the 1920s. The Crown, once owned by Cann and Clarke's Wymondham Brewery, was the stopping-point for coaches of the Telegraph Company in the nineteenth century. In the early 1970s it was converted into a youth centre. The trees on the left no longer hang over the street.

Queen's Square, the heart of Attleborough, in 1910. After the post office moved to Exchange Street in 1939, the building on the left became the Doric restaurant. Historic College House, behind the tree on the right, was demolished in 1972.

A cab is driven unhurriedly past Queen's Square in the early 1920s. Just visible behind a tree on the square is a German field gun, which had been placed there at the end of the First World War; when it had arrived at the railway station some young men had wanted to dump it in the Slaughterhouse Pond on Besthorpe Road! Later, it was moved to the west wall of College House and eventually it disappeared.

A view of Exchange Street at the turn of the century, with Queen's Road off to the right. In 1920 the war memorial was erected on the grass triangle. Behind the tree is Cyprus House, once a gentleman-farmer's abode, but later to become renowned for its tea gardens.

Queen's Road, c. 1908. The tall building, once the drill hall, was described by a visitor in 1896 as 'the Lilliputian Assembly Room tacked on to a row of neat little houses'. In the foreground, Evergreen Lodge had been built around 1860 by Robert Haselwood, a plumber, on a site where a blacksmith's shop had once stood.

Tranquil Chapel Road at the turn of the century. The building in the left foreground, which was once the 3Ms café, remains, but others, like the row of white cottages, are gone. On the right stood the Labour Exchange and, further down, the Salvation Army Hall.

The historic Cock Inn in 1908 when Charles Foulsham, a corn and coal merchant, was proprietor. The days when it was a posting inn of some importance are long since gone and the stores have also been demolished.

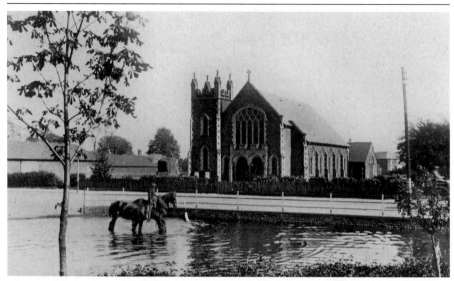

Rural Attleborough, *c.* 1918. Horses were watered at the Horse Pit before they went to the nearby blacksmith's shop. Much later, the pit was filled in to become a car park. To the left of the Primitive Methodist Chapel, erected in 1913, are buildings which were then part of Town Farm. For many years, up to the time he sold it in 1940, the farm was run by local worthy David Carlton, but the site is now covered by housing.

London Road looking very different at the turn of the century. Past the Horse Pit was the King's Head pub, which closed its doors soon after the picture was taken. Later, the building housed F. Smith and Company's motor repair business and then Mattie Ayton's newspaper shop. Jeremiah Reeve's smithy, one of several in the town, was behind.

Connaught Road in the 1920s. The thoroughfare was named after the Duke of Connaught, who visited the town around 1880. Around 1912, Robert McKelvie opened his outfitter's business in Connaught House, partly hidden by the trees on the right, and this flourished until 1987. The Oddfellows's pub can be seen on the left.

The Royal Hotel was once called the New Inn, but, after the Duke of Connaught was billeted there with his regiment (*c.* 1880), it was renamed the Royal. On the left was the 'Tap', where coachmen were accommodated; nearby Thieves Lane was once known as Tap Lane.

The Wesleyan Chapel stood in Station Road. It has been demolished long since and a veterinary practice stands on the site. The single-storey building at the front, which was once Clarke's confectionery and baker's shop, was also pulled down. Commemorating the peace of 1856, which ended the Crimean War, the obelisk was the work of Edward Robins, a stonemason from Wymondham.

The Station Road works of Anthony Harrison, builder, decorator and undertaker, *c.* 1910. The firm had been established in 1864. In 1916 it was advertising that 'the newest designs in paperhanging from the principal London Houses can be had at the shortest notice'.

The Station Hotel around 1910 when Francis Nobbs was the landlord. Attleborough boys, who attended Thetford Grammar School, stored their bicycles at the pub before boarding the train. Now it is called Soma House.

Jimmy Lee's hoarding at the Old Buckenham end of Station Road in 1913. The Wymondham bill poster was advertising not only the weekly sales of Attleborough auctioneers Salter and Simpson, but also Hethersett races and Wymondham shops.

Mrs Edith Bowles, wife of the proprietor William, and Charles Pooley, her father, standing outside the Old Railway Tavern in the 1920s. The pub stood nearer to the station than the New Railway Tavern and, between the two buildings, a lane ran to the mill. In 1904 it was advertising 'wagonettes, dog carts and ponies on hire'; and it also boasted a strong quoits team.

The New Railway Tavern on Station Road in 1908. In the 1920s the wife of the landlord Robert Thompson sold sweets from the front room on the right-hand side. A garage now stands on the site, while the mill at the back has also been demolished.

SECTION TWO
Wymondham Scenes

The historic Market Cross at the turn of the century. The cross was built in 1617–18 to replace what was probably an earlier Market Hall destroyed in the town's great fire of 1615. It was once used for meetings of the court, which administered the affairs of the market, and from about 1870 to 1912 served as a library and reading room. The buildings behind the Market Cross, on the right-hand corner of Queen's Street, included a group of fine Georgian houses but were demolished in a development in the early 1960s. In the street can be seen poles being transported from stacks on Norwich Road to the turnery of Robert Semmence & Sons at Cavick.

The impressive Georgian façade of the King's Head Inn, *c.* 1880. Standing on the Market Place, it was once the stopping-point for coaches and, for several hundred years, the principal social centre of the town. Closed in 1962, it was pulled down to make way for the Woolworth's store.

The post office in Market Street at the turn of the century. It had moved from the Market Place around 1896 and stayed there until 1940 when the new post office was opened in Middleton Street. After this the building housed the Mary Elizabeth Tea Rooms, but, when these closed in 1961, it was demolished and a supermarket built in its place.

Looking down an almost deserted Market Street in the 1890s. Behind the lamppost on the right can be seen Parkers' Supply Stores, which had been established in 1809. Renowned for their 'admirable sauces', Parkers sold virtually everything until a huge fire destroyed the store in September 1901.

St Thomas à Becket's Chapel in Church Street (formerly Churchgate Street), *c.* 1870. Founded in 1174, the chapel housed the Grammar School from 1559 to 1835 and again from 1888 to 1903. Until the mid-1800s, a gaol, fire-engine house and shops, one a fishmonger's, stood in front of the chapel. The shop of Robert Wright, saddler and harness maker, is on the right.

The fifteenth-century Green Dragon Inn makes a lovely backdrop to this winter scene at the turn of the century. One of the few buildings in the town to escape the great fire of 1615, it once may have been a hostelry for visitors to the abbey, and then one of the shops that three hundred years ago existed in Church Street.

Church Street looking towards Vicar Street in the late 1880s. A barn and cottages were being demolished to make way for various developments, including Larner House, which later became the Red House and eventually the Abbey Hotel. In 1919 an adjacent building became the Labour Institute, but it is now part of the hotel complex.

Picturesque Cavick in the 1890s captured by pioneer Wymondham photographer Henry Cushing. The cottages on the right have vanished long since, while one of those further down was once the home of 'Cocky' John Forster, a local character who was employed in digging ditches and driving cattle.

A view of Town Green from Middleton Street, looking very different in 1880. There was no Town Hall (now the Antiques Centre) and no war memorial, and the dwelling just past the shops at the end of Middleton Street was later strikingly altered to become Turret House.

Wymondham's first recreation ground around the time it opened in August 1909. It was situated on the site of the present Priory Gardens and post office, an area which up to 1903 had been the Grammar School's playground. Tennis courts and a bowling green were laid, while the Grammar School's gymnasium, seen in the background, was again put to its original use.

Stately Caius House, an early Georgian building, at the beginning of the century. When Charles Bird lived there in the 1930s a private bowling club played on the green at the rear, but in late 1933 the Revd F. Jarvis, the vicar, remarked that the house had been ruined by shop-fronts.

A 15 in shell which once stood on the Middleton Street corner outside Becket's Chapel. It had been presented to the town in appreciation of efforts made to raise money during the First World War. In 1932 the Parish Council considered a proposal that it was unsightly and should be removed. However, the British Legion stepped in to clean and polish it, so it remained, probably until the Second World War when there was a call for metal.

Incidents like this were once all too familiar in Damgate. This one occurred on a Saturday morning in May 1935 and held up traffic for two hours, the local press commenting that it emphasized the need for a bypass. However, that was not forthcoming until 1958.

A rare view of Damgate, *c.* 1880. The house on the extreme left was washed away in the 1912 floods, while the tall building, further up on the same side, was demolished to make way for old people's bungalows. The early seventeenth-century Sun Inn, once famous for its pleasure gardens by the river Tiffey, closed its doors in 1958.

Duffield's smithy in White Horse Street around 1887, the year it was established. In the early 1900s it was one of several operating in the town and continued to do so until 1935 when Duffield's engineering business moved to Silfield Road.

White Horse Street around 1912 – when you could stand in the road! James 'Jimmy' Lee, who had run a billposting business since 1880, lived in the house on the right. The cottages on the left in the background were demolished years ago.

Fairland Street, once known as Fairstead Street, in the early 1900s. The entrance to the then flourishing saleground can be seen on the right, but, since 1983, this has been the exit from the Health Centre, which was built on the saleground site. Just beyond now stands the Job Centre.

A fair on the Fairland in the 1890s. In his diary for 1892, Henry Cushing describes one such occasion when he mentions the Fairland as 'full of shows and stalls, steam horses, swing boats etc'. Just visible on the right is the corner of the Woolpack pub.

A hoar-frost makes a wintry scene at Station Road in early December 1925. In the background to the left is Browick Road School, while Browick Mill can be seen to the right. Soon after the picture was taken the mill's sails were blown off in a gale, though by that time it was no longer worked by wind.

Village Life

An outing in wagonettes at the Pelican pub in Tacolneston at the turn of the century. The picture was taken just after the Pelican, then a Steward & Patteson house, had changed its name from the Warren Arms. The Warren family formerly resided in Tacolneston Hall. Once a Forester's Lodge met regularly at the Pelican and it could be one of their outings which is seen here.

A rare photograph, taken around 1880, of Samuel Barrett's wine, spirit and ale stores in Queen's Road, Hethersett. Barrett also became a grocer and draper; and later, when the Buckinghams took over, the shop also became the post office.

A children's pageant at Hethersett in July 1924. It was enacted by children from the Sunday School of the Parish Church and staged in the beautiful grounds of Wood Hall. Ruby Nicholls was Old Mother Hubbard and several of the children on the right came from the Ringer family, including Percy (extreme right) and Daphne in front of him.

Cann's Lane at Hethersett in those lazy days of summer years ago. This picture was taken in 1920 and shows the lane looking quite different from today.

The smithy and cottages that once stood on the corner between the Wymondham–Bungay Road and the Norwich–New Buckenham Road at Ashwellthorpe. For about forty years at the turn of the century, William Mayes was the blacksmith and wheelwright, and the corner became known as Mayes's Corner. Now the buildings have gone, the listed cottages being demolished in 1984, and the corner is known as Smithy Corner.

A fête at Ashwellthorpe Hall in the early 1920s. Fêtes were an important feature of village life and this one made a profit of £140 for use in cleaning the churchyard. The hall dates from the Elizabethan period and at the time was the home of Major Leslie Fletcher.

The then isolated Primitive Methodist Chapel at Suton Street, soon after it was erected in 1889 to hold one hundred worshippers. One big event on the chapel calendar was the Sunday School anniversary; on that occasion in 1935 it was reported that the scholars 'acquitted themselves well in the delivery of their versed messages and the singing went with a swing'.

The original Three Boars public house at Spooner Row after it was seriously damaged by fire on a Sunday morning early in May 1926. It is shown after Edward Daines, the landlord who was also a blacksmith, had the remains tidied up and a corrugated iron roof added. Thereafter, the present Three Boars was built.

Gabriel Jackson, general shopkeeper, provided a useful delivery service from his 'cash stores' at Wymondham Road, Bunwell, when this picture was taken around 1916. The shop closed shortly before the Second World War and is now a private house.

The smithy on Bunwell Street in 1913 when run by Henry Soame. On the end facing the road, billposter 'Jimmy' Lee and his son Gus had a hoarding, which is seen advertising Wendling sports, sales and various Wymondham shops. The smithy ceased operating after the Second World War and it has been pulled down long since.

Looking across the wide expanse of New Buckenham Square just after the turn of the century. The three-storey all-purpose shop of W.N. Austin, grocer and draper, was destroyed in a disastrous fire (see page 110). The sixteenth-century Market House, just one of many architectural gems in the village, saw punishments meted out at its central whipping-post, which still survives complete with arm clamps.

The New Buckenham Silver Band on parade in the village in 1921. The band was founded in 1887 and made its first public appearance to help with Queen Victoria's Golden Jubilee celebrations in that year. Since then the band has become something of an institution in South Norfolk, and, indeed, further afield, and it has played for many occasions from concerts and fêtes to British Legion parades and Agricultural Workers Union rallies.

The Crown Inn at Old Buckenham around 1910 when it was a Bullard's house. It was one of many such pubs essential to village life, and replaced an earlier inn of the same name which stood on Crown Road. On the edge of the green, the Crown is now called the Ox and Plough – and the hitch-rail is no longer there!

Wicklewood Mill in 1912. William Wade, the miller, with two of his sons, Wilfrid and Dennis on the right, in the cart pulled by Kitty the horse. This five-storey tower corn mill was built around 1845, but milling ceased in 1942. In 1977 Margaret Edwards, daughter of Dennis, handed the mill over to the Norfolk Windmills Trust and it has since been restored.

Horses and carts outside the new Deopham public elementary school in Vicarage Road in 1924, the year it was built. It was erected to replace a corrugated iron structure which had only been erected in 1909 and is still standing in another part of the village. In the early years of the new school, the mistress was Ada Hart; she was later awarded the BEM for Red Cross and political services in Wymondham. The school became redundant in 1980 and is now a private house.

Staff posing outside the Morley St Botolph post office and village shop, *c.* 1915. The girl with the bicycle was employed to deliver telegrams. At the time it was run by John L. Barttrum and letters arrived and were dispatched through Wymondham post office. The business closed in 1991.

A Crisp's coach stops to pick up passengers outside the White Hart pub in the Market Place at Hingham. In the late 1920s and through the 1930s these coaches, which were coloured green, ran a service between Northwold and All Saint's Green in Norwich. In the nineteenth century the petty sessions were held at the White Hart, which had been a coaching inn of some importance.

Preston's dairy in the Market Place at Hingham in 1931. John Preston is on the left and the other man is John Muttit. The dairy stood opposite the White Hart and is now a newsagents. Note the advert for the 'Pink Un' or 'Eastern Football News', put there by the papershop which was next door.

Hingham festivities in August 1913 when a granite memorial stone was presented from the inhabitants of Hingham in Massachusetts, USA. Samuel Lincoln, an ancestor of Abraham Lincoln, emigrated to America in 1637 from Hingham. In 1919 John Davis, the American ambassador, unveiled a bust of Abraham Lincoln in Hingham Church.

SECTION FOUR

School-days

The Primitive Methodist Sunday School outing at Attleborough in June 1905. Leaving the town by Queen's Road, the destination of these annual outings by wagonette seemed to be either a farmer's meadow at Great Ellingham, where games and a tea would be enjoyed, or the Loch Neaton pleasure gardens near Watton. In 1908 over one hundred children went to Loch Neaton, where boating was popular.

Wicklewood School in 1928. On the right is Bertram Topham, the headmaster. Children from the nearby Poor Law Institution attended the school, one such boy being seen second from the right in the back row and distinguishable by his roll-neck pullover. Generally, village and workhouse children mixed well together at school, but saw little of each other outside.

The Wymondham Board School on Browick Road in 1893, when the boys were kept separate from the girls. The headmaster was Richard Shockley, a strict disciplinarian and probably the man with the beard. When the school opened in 1876, it catered for 180 boys, 180 girls and 200 infants.

The Council Schools at Attleborough in 1910. They had been erected in 1840, and enlarged in 1895. On the right in the foreground is the garden of the headmaster's house. Cookery and woodwork classes were held in the building on the right, but girls, boys and infants were taught separately.

The manual room at Attleborough Council School, c. 1910. Here, the girls undertook cookery and sometimes laundry, while the boys learnt woodwork.

A class from Browick Road School, Wymondham, at the town's swimming bath in the early 1930s. The bath was opened in July 1931 by William Smith, who is shown on the left of the picture, in the premises of a former brewery. The huge beer vat was used as a pool! On the opening day the Heigham Penguin Swimming Club gave a diving display, and in the following years many clubs from Norwich and the surrounds patronized the pool. The bath closed in 1953 and part of the premises later housed the headquarters of the South Norfolk Labour Party. The man in the centre at the back is William 'Shag' Baker, who taught at the school from 1919 until retirement in 1958, by which time he had instructed over fifteen thousand pupils. His nickname was derived from the tobacco he smoked.

The Wymondham Central Boys School team who won the Primary Shield for Norfolk Schools in the 1909–10 season. Mr J. Sparkes, the headmaster, is behind the shield and the teacher kneeling on the right is Leslie Barnard. Among the team, in the middle row are extreme left W. Middleton and third from left Leslie Kerridge.

The victorious Wymondham Grammar School cricket team of the 1890s. In 1891 the school defeated a strong Paston Grammar School side, in the final at Lakenham, by nine wickets to take the Norwich Schools' Shield. Returning to Wymondham, the victors were carried from the railway station in style in a wagonette.

The boys of the Attleborough Council School constructing a sunken rose garden in the school grounds, *c.* 1932. In the 1930s the school became renowned for its garden, the master for the subject being Jimmy Reed, who is seen standing in front of the sixth lad from the right on the back row. Mr Lionel Twiddy (headmaster) is holding the urn, while Mrs Twiddy (headmistress) can be seen at the back.

Attleborough Council School girls on the playing field, *c.* 1908. Both the Cock Meadow and the Royal Meadow were used by the school for sporting activities.

The annual 'bun fight' for the sons of Attleborough Oddfellows, held in the Corn Hall, c. 1930. The officials sporting their chains of office stand at the back. The Oddfellows were particularly strong in Attleborough and, at the time, the Lodge met at the Bear Hotel, the secretary being Bertram Turner.

Browick Road schoolchildren dancing round the maypole on the King's Head Meadow at Wymondham on 6 May 1935. Always a popular school activity, the dancing actually pictured was to celebrate the Silver Jubilee of King George V. In the background can be seen the roof of the old tithe barn.

Boys at Morley St Botolph are proud of the snowman which they made at school on a winter day around 1910. The photograph was actually taken by their headmaster, Mr Thomas Ormond.

Some Wymondham Cubs taking a drink on the Abbey Meadows at Whitsun 1932. The man at the back is Fred 'Paddy' Parsons, who was a Cub instructor and prominent Scout patrol leader at the time. In 1931 he had been awarded a medal for saving a life at Wymondham swimming bath on its opening day.

The Workplace

Wymondham brushmaker William Carter (third from the left in the back row) with some of his employees and family, *c*. 1913. Formerly employed by S.D. Page & Sons, the brushmakers, he set up his own business in Market Street in 1908, moving it to the former Dove public house in Town Green five years later. The business flourished until the Second World War.

The Briton Brush Company's factory at Wymondham in its heyday, *c.* 1930. It was in 1890 that the Norwich brushmakers S.D. Page & Sons erected the factory at Lady's Lane, though at the time they also had a bass dressing and drafting works in Cann's old brewery in Brewery Lane. Soon after the picture was taken, the cottages facing the White Horse pub were demolished to increase the capacity of the factory's machine room. Following an amalgamation in 1920, the firm became the Briton Brush Company and later, after further changes in name, the factory was closed in 1985. Now a housing estate stands on the site, but the brushmaking tradition, established by S.D. Page & Sons, survives at Attleborough with Hamilton Acorn Limited, their descendants, who make fine paint brushes.

The Briton Brush Company's siding in the late 1940s. Opened in 1916, the siding was busy receiving raw materials like African bass and Mexican fibres, while dispatching the finished brushes. Every lunch-time, a shunting-engine from Wymondham station assisted with the operation.

The Briton Brush sawmills at Wymondham, c. 1950. Here the brush handles are being moulded. The young man is Harry Boughen.

The sand room of the Briton Brush factory, *c.* 1950. The girls are busy smoothing handles. In the foreground on the left are Ivy Cowles and Mabel Woodbine; the first girl on the right is Kitty Brown.

The Briton Brush 'making' shop decorated to celebrate the 1937 coronation of George VI. It was here that the heads of paint brushes were fixed to the handles. Hilda Cooper is the lady in front looking straight into the camera.

The Co-operative Wholesale Society's factory at Chapel Lane, Wymondham, shortly before its demolition in 1987–8 to make way for a housing estate. Opened in 1922, at its height it employed 220 people, but closed for good in January 1983.

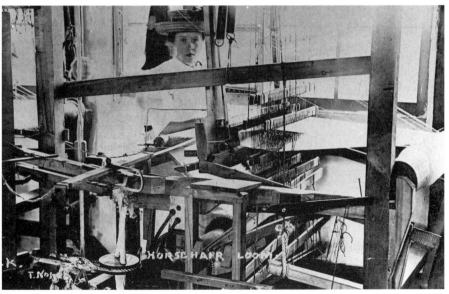

The inside of Hovell & Co.'s horsehair weaving factory at Friarscroft Lane, Wymondham, at the turn of the century. In 1836 there were six hundred looms in the town, but by the time of the picture the trade was in decline. However, the name Rattle Row still reminds us of the noisy looms.

Gaymer's cider factory at Attleborough, *c.* 1910. The firm had its origins at Banham, but William Gaymer moved it to Attleborough in 1896 to be near the railway. The buildings have undergone extensive alterations since the picture was taken and the chimney was demolished after a taller chimney was built around 1930. At one time the factory employed several hundred people at Attleborough, but now only about forty-five work there.

The cooper's shop at Gaymer's. On the left Philip Smith and Horace Lancaster are repairing a 140 gallon butt, Tom Gedge in the middle is branding casks, while Jimmy Gedge is repairing a pipe (a cask for 105 gallons). The pieces of cloth hanging up in the background were for wiping leaking casks.

Shovelling apples into a mill for grinding to pulp before transfer to the pressing operation. The man on the right is Sid Blackburn.

Using a hand-press at Gaymer's in the 1940s. Coconut matting and ash slats were part of the make-up of such presses. The operator is Charlie Styles.

The railway sidings at Gaymer's factory in the 1930s. Cases of bottled cider are being loaded on to trucks for transportation from the factory. The tall building in the background housed the hoist for raising bags of apples. The man nearest the camera, in the wagon, is George Mace. On the left are crates of second-hand champagne bottles used for Pometta Cider.

A 1930s advert for two-gallon jars of cider, and the front of a 1911 price list.

Dinner-time in the harvest field at Attleborough Hall Farm in 1931. In the front is Joe Parker with his children Kitty, Josy and Cecil. The youngsters used the pram on the right to take dinner to the men working in the fields. Beer or cider was drunk from stone jars.

Threshing at Potash Farm, Hethel, c. 1906. The man standing at the front wearing a straw boater is John Rowe and next to him is his son Edgar.

Robert John Plunkett, nearest the camera, with other members of his family in the forge at the turn of the century. Plunketts started repairing bicycles, but then became agricultural engineers in their workshop, which was situated at the corner of Back Lane and Bridewell Street, Wymondham. In the 1940s the business was taken over by Boddy's (agricultural) Limited and later by Gurney Reeve & Co. Ltd.

Digging a trench in those labour intensive days at the beginning of the century. The men are in the road by Cherry Row, Attleborough, and they are probably helping to lay gas pipes.

John Wick and Son's delivery lorry in the early 1920s. The driver was Sid Lake and the firm had their yard off Station Road, Attleborough. In 1918 they described themselves as 'corn, cake, seed, salt, coal and coke merchants, millers and manufacturers of standard flour'.

Wymondham Laundry staff at their Norwich Road depot in the 1930s. Sixth from the left and sporting a bow-tie is Allen Dodman, the manager, who retired after twenty-one years service in 1941. When the laundry closed in 1969, the buildings were demolished and a supermarket built. Now the store too has been taken down and houses stand on the site.

Men at work in a Wymondham stone pit, *c.* 1910. In the late nineteenth century it was Charles Ayton who realized the importance of Wymondham flints for road-making and set up a business, which at its height saw two hundred men employed in pits around the locality. However, with the arrival of other materials, the stone pits closed.

Some of Ayton's staff at their Browick Road works in 1932. With the decline in the demand for flints, the firm developed other products like bitumen and hottrin, and today the Ayton Asphalt Company still survives. Fifth from left in the picture is Cecil Atherton, who rose from office boy to managing director.

Looking down the High Street towards Connaught Plain, Attleborough, in the 1920s when the traffic was much quieter. The buildings further down on both sides are no longer there. The shop with the canopy is Prince's Army and Navy Stores, while wireless accumulators could be handed in at Pickrell's for recharging.

The Town Green emporium of J.R. Smith & Son at Wymondham in 1909. The man in the doorway is William Jermyn Smith, son of the founder John Robert, and the small child is Clifford, William's five-year-old son. The business was established in 1857 and closed in 1911 on William's death. Much later, Hubert Corston kept the shop and now it is called the Village Store.

The International Stores in Church Street, Attleborough, c. 1910. It had been established in the town about five years earlier and for a long time was the principal grocery shop, its van delivering orders to surrounding villages. The trade bicycle, seen on the left, was also used for taking out orders. The lady sixth from the left is Edith Pooley (later Bowles), the cashier, and the other lady is May Viney (later Mrs Rix).

The all-purpose store of Clarke & Co. in Market Street, Wymondham, *c.* 1905. Founded in 1881 by Edward 'Ginger' Clarke, it was sited on the corner now occupied by Geo. R. Reeve Limited, which became known as 'Clarke's Corner'. With the death of the proprietor Harry Clarke in 1969, the store closed.

The Spooner Row village shop was vital to the local community when this picture was taken around 1912. George Wharton ran it for over fifty years from around 1870 and was succeeded by his brother Thomas. It sold groceries, drapery and meat, baked its own bread and acted as the post office. Much of this had changed by the time it closed for good in March 1990.

The High Street at Attleborough looking towards London Road, *c.* 1914. At the entrance to Hargham Road, Le Grice's grocery and drapery has since had a succession of owners. Later Lambert's cycle depot became Prince's Army and Navy Stores, while the opening by the lamppost led to the Cock Meadow. Here on the last Thursday in March was held the Rogues' fair, so called because it fell at a time when prisoners were being conveyed in open wagons from Norwich to the assizes at Thetford.

Edward Warne, grocer, draper and general dealer, outside his stores on the Lizard at Wymondham, *c.* 1910. Once the Lizard also boasted a fish-curing business and George Stubb's steam bakery and grocery. Stubb's shop was taken over by the Percival family and it closed in 1962.

Clarence Matthews's shop in Church Street with a display for a special occasion promoting the virtues of fish in pre-war Attleborough. Set up in the 1920s, Matthews's sold both fish and fruit. Today the Wood family, who took over the shop around 1963, offer wet fish and fish and chips.

Charles Dye's 'hygienic' bakery at Attleborough in the 1920s. Later, it became Mitchell's and then the Sunshine Bread store. Now a snooker hall stands on the London Road site.

Wearing his apron, Edward Blyth is standing in the doorway of his family's baker's and grocer's in Friarscroft Lane, Wymondham, *c.* 1925. The other man in the picture is Ernest Stubbs, a flamboyant character who lived in a nearby cottage, while the notice behind him was advertising a film featuring Rin Tin Tin, the silent screen's wonder dog, at the town's Picture House in Town Green. Friarscroft Lane residents also enjoyed the services of a general stores run by George Harwood, who delivered locally by horse and trolley.

George 'Cutty' Segger stands outside his confectionery shop on Queen's Square, Attleborough, in 1946. Later, one of his daughters, Millie, opened a bric-à-brac business there.

The butcher's shop of Edward Parsons (extreme right) on Connaught Plain, Attleborough, *c.* 1909. The man second from left is Frank Myhill and the boy is Harold Parsons. By 1925 the business had moved to London Road and Harold was running it.

Tuddenham's butcher's shop in Town Green, Wymondham, *c.* 1906. The family business had been established for over one hundred years when the shop was taken over by John Wharton on William Tuddenham's death in 1914. Wharton had already opened a shop in Damgate in 1890, so for a time ran two shops, but the business finally moved to Market Street in 1938, before closure in 1990. The Youngs Crawshay and Youngs sign is on the wall of the neighbouring Leather Bottle pub, which closed around the time the photograph was taken.

Clements and Sons' shop on Wymondham Market Place, at the corner with Bridewell Street, *c.* 1910. This old family ironmongery had been established in Fairland Street in the 1870s. The additional Market Place premises were acquired around 1890 and ran until the early 1920s when Clements reverted solely to the Fairland Street shop.

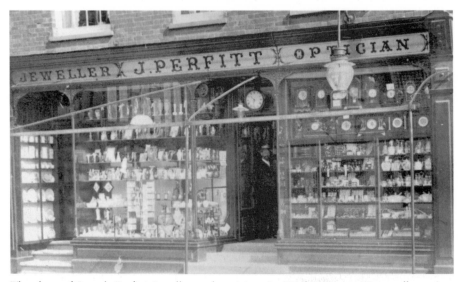

The shop of Joseph Perfitt, jeweller and optician, in Market Street, Wymondham, just before Gurney Wade took it over around 1910. Gurney Wade, a well-known local photographer, ran a gift shop until the early 1930s when he sold out to A.W. Gibbs, who continued the business until 1953. Later, Cooke's shoe shop and a coffee shop occupied the premises.

Frederick Youngs, a monumental mason, was running this quaint little shop in Queen's Road, Attleborough, before the Second World War. The workshop and stone yard were at the rear of the shop. The family business had been established in 1867 and by 1904 George Youngs was conducting it in Connaught Road premises.

Members of the Standley family pose outside Ye Olde Curiosity Shop in Wymondham Market Place in the 1920s. Originating in Pople Street, the family business moved to the Market Place around 1917 and flourished until the late 1960s. Herbert Standley is in the right-hand doorway and Arthur Standley in the other.

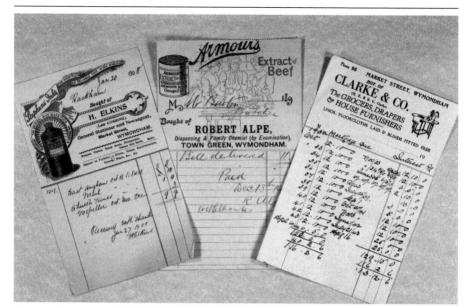

Wymondham shop bills.

Receipts from Attleborough traders.

Events

Queen Victoria's Diamond Jubilee celebrations at Wymondham in June 1897. Local worthies and the town band head a procession of nine hundred children down Damgate to the brush factory of S.D. Page & Sons, where they sat down to tea. George Williamson, a tailor and outfitter, was the man with the stick and Robert V. Reyner led the procession. Mr Reyner, who died in 1933, was active in numerous organizations in the town.

King Edward VII's cavalcade passes before the patriotic townsfolk of Wymondham on Monday 25 October 1909. The king had been staying with the Earl and Countess of Albemarle at Quidenham Hall and was on his way to Norwich. Businesses were closed so employees could cheer the monarch, and local schoolchildren were marched to the Market Place where they joined the Abbey choir to sing the national anthem as His Majesty passed by.

For the king's visit to Attleborough, Queen's Square had been reserved for the schoolchildren from the town and neighbouring villages. The town had been 'prettily' decorated and the road was thronged with cheering crowds. Afterwards the schoolchildren were provided with refreshments.

St Mary's Church choir, Attleborough, who took part in a divine service to celebrate George V's coronation on 22 June 1911. The group are posing outside the old Rectory and the Rector, the Revd Maxwell Webb, is the clergyman on the right of the middle. Mrs Webb sits in the middle.

Decorated floats representing various parts of the empire were the theme of Attleborough's coronation procession in 1911. However, the town's festivities were marred by rival committees bringing out competing programmes, and a large gathering found a schoolchildren's display on the Point House Meadow more of an attraction than the parade.

The scene at Abbotsford, Wymondham, on coronation day 1911. Capt. H.L. Cautley had invited the schoolchildren to the beautiful grounds of his home where they enjoyed tea, having earlier taken part in rural sports on the King's Head Meadow. Each child received a coronation mug.

The tea tent makes a leisurely scene at Hethersett's coronation celebrations in July 1911. Owing to 'the difficulty in catering for so large a village', the festivities had been postponed from 22 June. After the celebrations were paid for, the remaining £2 was handed over to the Hethersett Sick and Needy fund.

This bonfire was lit in the evening to conclude Old Buckenham's coronation day celebrations in 1911. Earlier, there had been a parish dinner, children's tea, sports and a firework display. A band provided music throughout the day.

Scouts, Cubs and other organizations assembled in Wymondham Market Place for a St George's Day parade in 1934. Behind are the once popular shops of the Norwich Co-operative Society.

At Attleborough the most spectacular of many events to celebrate George V's Silver Jubilee, on 6 May 1935, was the grand parade. Seen here coming up Queen's Road, the procession toured the town, which was described as 'the best decorated place between Epping and Norwich'.

In the Wymondham Silver Jubilee celebrations of 1935, Bobby Youngman took first prize in the children's fancy dress parade; he featured Gaymer's cider from Attleborough!

The crowning of Lily Lee as queen for Wymondham's first carnival in 1936. The lady performing the honours is Mrs Ethel Boileau, a celebrated novelist of the time. The three attendants are (left to right): Vivian Jones, Alice Harrison and Margery Duffield, while the gentlemen on the right are Edwin Gooch, the chairman of the Urban District Council, and George Reeve, Grand Marshall of the Carnival Procession. Colonel Raymond Boileau is on the left.

At Attleborough's coronation parade in May 1937, David Carlton (seen with trilby) won first prize in the decorated horse-drawn vehicles class. Mr Carlton, once a horse dealer, farmed Town Farm for thirty-five years until he sold it in 1940. He died in 1976, aged 99.

The annual Briton Brush employees' outing gets ready to leave Wymondham station, *c.* 1935. On this occasion they were bound for Skegness and those standing on the front of the engine are (left to right): Hilda Cooper, Molly Nobbs and Edgar Bilner, who looked after the factory boilers.

Fun on the King's Head Meadow at an athletic sports meeting in the late 1940s. The man in the clown's garb is legendary Wymondham character Alf Harvey, who is probably best remembered further afield as a Norwich City FC mascot. In the background can be seen the old Wymondham Town football pavilion, now replaced by a modern clubhouse. (Photograph by courtesy of Eastern Counties Newspapers Ltd.)

Attleborough's famous Michaelmas Turkey Sale in the early 1950s. St Edmund's old people's home now stands on the site where auctions were conducted by the old established firm of Salter Simpson & Sons. Weekly sales, which included a range of livestock, were held at the ground, but it was the annual 'Turkey Day' at Michaelmas that, with Gaymer's cider, made Attleborough famous. Cottagers, small farmers and large breeders would bring their birds in tumbrils and donkey carts, later vans and lorries. Several thousand 'gobblers' were displayed in neat wire netting pens stretching in rows the length of the field. Many turkeys were bought for the big London stores and for provision merchants around the country.

Turkeys being driven from the saleground to the railway station after being sold at the annual Michaelmas Fair in the 1920s. They did not mind walking, but they hated hurrying.

A 1940s scene at Wymondham's weekly livestock sales. Among those grading cattle are Mr Palmer, auctioneer with cap on the left, Tom Wharton, butcher with white coat, and Jimmy Standley, third from right with cap. Cattle, sheep and pigs were once driven down Fairland Street to the saleground, which was on the site afterwards occupied by the Health Centre.

SECTION EIGHT

Sport and Leisure

The Wymondham and District Miniature Rifle Club in 1914. The club was founded in 1911 and Fred Roope (back row, extreme left) was to be its honorary secretary for about forty-five years. For a long time the range was in gravel pits at Browick Road, which later became the recreation ground. Among those pictured in the back row are: Sergeant Webster (second from left), Fred Bird (third from left), J.B. Pomeroy (fourth from left and club captain) and Captain H.L. Cautley (fifth from left).

A cycling event at one of Wymondham's annual Whit Thursday athletic sports meetings on the King's Head Meadow in the 1890s. The sports enjoyed an unrivalled reputation throughout East Anglia and there was dismay when they were dropped in 1909. However, they were revived in 1912, albeit on a restricted basis, and well-organized meetings were still being held in the early 1950s.

The front cover of the programme of the third athletic sports held under the auspices of the sporting clubs of Attleborough. Three thousand spectators enjoyed the events, the highlight being the 2 mile flat race, recognized by the Amateur Athletic Association and won for the second successive year by J.B. Greenwood, the Attleborough runner.

The Attleborough Bear Hotel bowls team, which won the Wymondham and District League at its first attempt in 1927. Previously, the 'Bears' had played in the South Norfolk League. The team included G.S. Youngs and David Carlton who are shown fourth and fifth from the left in the back row.

Prize Day at the Sun Inn Bowling Club at Wymondham in 1902. Mr W.L. Boyle, later Conservative and Unionist MP for Mid Norfolk, is sitting beside the table holding his bowler. For years, the Sun was renowned for its picturesque green beside the river Tiffey and was one of several clubs in the town.

Attleborough Town FC in the 1908/9 season when they met with little success. Winning only three fixtures, the team finished third from the bottom in the strong Norwich District League and a proposed amalgamation with Gaymers FC was declined by the factory. At the time they were probably playing on the Cock Meadow.

Attleborough FC's successful Allerton Cup team in the 1951/2 season. Captain John Fuller holds the cup, which they won when they beat East Harling 3–2 at Diss in the final. The goalkeeper is Bob Myhill. (Photograph by courtesy of Eastern Counties Newspapers Ltd.)

Wymondham Town FC's team of the late 1950s when two exciting runs were enjoyed in the FA Amateur Cup. The highlight came in October 1958 with a 4–3 win over Yarmouth Town on the King's Head Meadow. Ken Percival (sitting second left), the town's finest all-round sportsman, scored nine goals in a 15–2 league win over Thorpe in January 1957.

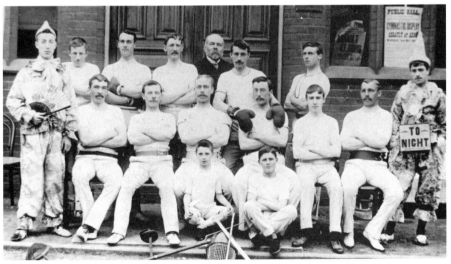

The participants in a gymnastic display at the Wymondham Town Hall (now the Antiques Centre), c. 1910. They were probably members of the club which had been set up by Charlie Cranness, in 1909, in the old Grammar School gymnasium near Back Lane.

Attleborough's formidable hockey team of the late 1930s. The picture, taken at School Lane, Thorpe, shows three prominent sporting brothers of the Cant family: Reggie (back row, extreme left), Arnold (back row, third left) and John (front row, second left).

Old Buckenham Hall epitomized country house cricket in the early 1900s. Australian financier Lionel Robinson (facing camera in left foreground), built a new Old Buckenham Hall in 1906, after pulling down the old one, and then laid a wonderful cricket pitch. He employed veteran England batsman, Archie MacLaren (seen with cap behind Robinson) as his cricket manager and staged big show matches, which attracted huge crowds. None was bigger than that in which an England XI met the touring Australian test side in 1921.

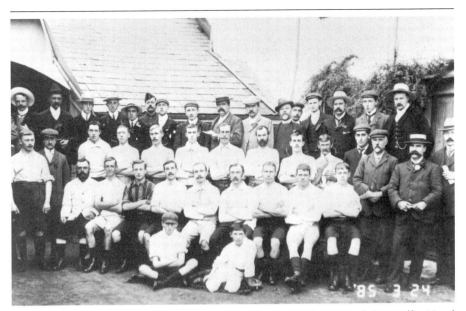

Officials and competitors in a walking match, pictured in the yard of the Griffin Hotel at Attleborough at the turn of the century. The walk was from Larlingford to Queen's Square, and the winner was Charles Sturman, who is the competitor on the right in the middle row.

Tennis clubs abounded in Wymondham in the 1930s and one of the strongest was that of the Congregational Church, seen here. Their courts were in Back Lane on the site now occupied by Standley Court. On the left are George Chapman and Eva Wharton (who married in 1933), while Bessie Taylor (later Cushion) is kneeling on the right.

A 1928 scene showing Wymondham's first swimming bath! Before the days of pollution the little river Tiffey was dammed on the Oxford Common to make a pool. It was Major H.L. Cautley from Abbotsford who probably first encouraged children in this practice, so they could learn to swim. In the picture are Peggy and Harry Tunaley.

The quoits team from the Eight Ringers' public house at Hingham in the 1920s. Quoits was a popular pub game and this photograph was taken in the Ringers' yard. Jimmy Thurston, the landlord, is in the middle of the front row with the boy, while among others are Billy Cooper (back row, third from left) and Ted Vincent wearing the bowler.

A production of *A Midsummer Night's Dream* at an Attleborough fête in July 1908. The fête was held in the Rectory grounds to raise money for the church restoration fund. In the evening a concert at the Church Hall included recitations by Miss Kate Gaymer.

Attleborough's Radio Dance Band, with Percy Armstrong on drums and leader Gerry Lee playing the violin, in the 1920s when the band was founded. As the Gerry Lee Band, it became the resident outfit at the Lido (later the Norwood Rooms) in Norwich and supported such well-known names as Roy Fox and Ambrose. They played at country house parties and even at the Hilton Hotel, but it all came to an end with the outbreak of the Second World War.

Mr William Spalding, proprietor, outside his Picture House in Town Green, Wymondham, in 1932. The building was opened as a Public Hall in 1889 and used for dramatic productions, operatic performances, dances, political rallies and many more functions. Silent films were shown from 1917 and Mr Spalding took it over in 1929, running the cinema until it closed in 1940.

Whist at Wymondham. Whist drives were a popular pastime and this outdoor one was held on the lawn of St Becket's House, Middleton Street, where Mr and Mrs J.W. Underwood lived. It was one of the events in the town's coronation celebrations of June 1953.

Transporting Christmas turkeys from Stanfield, near Wymondham, to the London market in 1913. Approximately 7 tons of rough-plucked turkeys in hampers were conveyed on a dray pulled by a traction-engine, and the round delivery time to the capital took about a week! It was John G. Peele, living at Stanfield Hall Farm, who began sending turkeys to London in 1880. Ernest Peele carried on the business and later his son Frank continued it at Downham Grove, before moving it to a farm at Thuxton, where Norfolk Black turkeys are still bred.

Some of the Wymondham railway station employees around 1906 when the station was in its heyday. Built with Brandon flints and red bricks, the station began its working life on 30 July 1845 when the line, constructed by the Norwich and Brandon Railway Company, was opened between the two places. At Brandon the line joined with the Eastern Counties Railway to provide a through link to London. Later in the year there was a merger with the Yarmouth and Norwich Railway to form the Norfolk Railway, and in 1846 special excursions were being run from Wymondham to Yarmouth with a fare of 3*d* (1p) return. A branch line to Dereham was opened for goods traffic in December 1846, and for passengers early the following year. Extensions to Fakenham and Wells followed. Then in May 1881 the line to Forncett via Ashwellthorpe, colloquially known as the 'Swede and Swimmer', was opened. This completed Wymondham's position as an important junction. Passenger services to Forncett stopped in September 1939, but it was after the Beeching Axe of the early 1960s that passenger traffic ended on the Dereham line in 1969. Now, the station is an unmanned halt, but local businessman David Turner has restored the buildings and turned them into a nostalgic tourist attraction.

Some of the uniformed railwaymen who worked at Wymondham station in 1920. Second from right is G.W. 'Wilfred' Coleman. The board at the back emphasizes Wymondham's importance as a junction. The station kept a pair of horses for moving waggons, and also had one for taking parcels to local shops and factories.

The staff of Attleborough station in the 1920s. In the middle of the front row is Frederick Hillier, then the long-serving stationmaster, and sitting with him are the goods and booking-office clerks. The station had an extensive goods shed and yard with sidings, and employed several shunting horses. As at Wymondham, its story had started with the opening of the Norwich and Brandon Railway in July 1845.

With an early 'Claud Hamilton' class engine pulling it, a local train stops at Spooner Row station. This was a frequent sight around the time the picture was taken in the early 1930s. Built of flints and red bricks in 1844, the station building, on the left, has been demolished. A stationmaster and two porters once manned the stop.

Like many coal merchants, Wick & Son at Attleborough had their own trucks and sidings. One lady, who lived as a girl in the railway cottages, recalls that because of coal dust, she was never allowed to change into her school uniform until it was actually time to leave for school.

Gertie Lowne (left) and Nora Chapman (later Dommer) at the counter of the refreshment room at Wymondham station in June 1925. Tea was about 3*d* (1p) a cup and the girls worked a six-day week from 7a.m. to 10p.m.

On a day in 1924, the 1.25p.m. train from Norwich, drawn by a 'Claud Hamilton' class engine, eases into Wymondham station, past the bookstall of W.H. Smith & Son Limited. Newspapers were delivered to the town from the bookstall and when Mrs Kate Ayers, a cheery character, was manageress after the Second World War, she worked a 6.15a.m. to 5.30p.m. day.

A train from Norwich draws into Attleborough station in the early 1950s. The large wooden store for corn and animal feeds, run by Brooks Mistley, was a familiar landmark.

Just before the First World War horse-drawn cabs as well as early motor cars were meeting trains at Wymondham station. Charles Mallows, then later his daughters Minnie and Kitty, and the King's Head Inn, both sent cabs to meet every train, the fare to town being 1s (5p). Charles Miles was cabman for the Mallows, who kept a Temperance Hotel in Middleton Street, and later Clifford Houchin drove for the King's Head, who progressed to motor taxis. A regular passenger was the Earl of Kimberley.

Jonathan Corston's cart delivering lemonade and ginger beer around the Wymondham locality early in the century. It was Jonathan who set up the firm of J. Corston & Co. and, having bought the aerated water business of George Tattam of Attleborough in 1898, moved the operation to Bunwell. Four years later he purchased the mineral water factory of Parker & Son at Browick Road, Wymondham (where now stands a dairy depot) and moved the firm there.

Early in the century, deliveries by Parsons, the Attleborough butchers, were made with pony and trap or on a trade bicycle. Taken on the Cock Meadow, the picture shows Edward 'Ted' Parsons with his son Harold in the middle. The man on the left on the cart is Frank Myhill.

The smart delivery van of Barwell & Sons, wine merchants of Wymondham, in 1932. A lady driver was not common in those days, but Mary Carter did the job for Barwells. Light and dark Tolly ales were 8s 6d (42½p) for a dozen pint bottles at this time. Barwells's shop was in the building which is now the South Norfolk District Labour Party headquarters.

New delivery vans for J. Corston & Co. outside the Norwich Road garage at Wymondham of Herbert Semmence and Company in the 1920s. At that time, Wesley Corston introduced the fleet of motorized vans, which toured the area advertising Weston-Thomas beverages on the side. Weston was a combination of Wesley and Corston, while Thomas was the Christian name of Mr Large of Diss. The soft drinks business closed in 1977.

A Model T Ford outside Ernest Smith & Sons' London Road Motor Garage at Attleborough around 1912, the year the neighbouring Albemarle Terrace was built. The firm had been established in 1909 and operated public service vehicles for fifty-three years to 1980. The building is now used for selling tyres.

Two Bullnose Morrises stop for petrol at Mr H. Ponder's filling station at Fettel Bridge, London Road, Attleborough, in the early 1930s. The petrol had to be cranked up and Mr Ponder is the man with the trilby. The Stag Inn now stands on the site.

A Norfolk Coachways outing in the halcyon excursion days of the 1930s. Pioneer coach operator John C. Brown first registered his Attleborough business as Norfolk Coachways in 1926, though he had started with a converted lorry about nine years earlier. The firm closed in 1992 after Mrs M.E. Eke, Brown's daughter, had run it for the last twenty years following his death. Sydney Sparrow, the firm's longest-serving driver, is shown on the extreme right in the back row.

Employees of the Friarscroft Laundry on Wymondham Market Place ready to depart in two of Semmence's charabancs on their annual outing in the 1920s. In 1923 they enjoyed a visit to Sandringham and Hunstanton, while in 1924 they were taken to Felixstowe. They were accompanied by Mr R.C. Rudrum, the head of the firm.

People

Agricultural labourers marching down Wicklewood High Street to Kimberley Park on Monday 16 April 1923 during the agricultural workers 'Great Strike'. Principally taking action against wage reductions, they had been to Wicklewood Workhouse to demand relief and food from the guardians and were then on their way to a big meeting at Kimberley Park, where the Earl of Kimberley, the first peer to declare himself a Labour Party supporter, took the chair. The man with the cap, standing on the left of the bicycle, is Herbert Coldham, and on the right with the trilby and bow-tie is Edwin Gooch, who is featured on the next page.

A meeting of the Norwich branch of the Amalgamated Society of Railway Servants on Wymondham Market Hill. Founded in 1871, the ASRS joined with other rail unions in 1913 to form the National Union of Railwaymen. The meeting was probably in 1911 at the time of the first national rail strike and it emphasized Wymondham's importance as a railway junction.

Labour legend George Edwards, on the right, with his agent Edwin Gooch outside the Labour Institute at Wymondham in August 1920. Mr Edwards had just won a stunning by-election victory to become MP for South Norfolk. Edwin Gooch, arguably Wymondham's most famous son after the rebellious Ketts, became President of the National Union of Agricultural Workers from 1928 to 1961 and MP for North Norfolk for many years.

The gathering at the opening of the Attleborough Liberal Club in Connaught House on 27 September 1911. The ceremony was performed by Mr W.R. Lester, the prospective parliamentary candidate. Previously, Connaught House had been the home of Miss Mary Kidner's ladies school and a shop. The Liberals moved their club to Queen's Square premises a year later, then Robert McKelvie opened his outfitters in Connaught House.

Gaymer's Football Club, who won the South Norfolk League in 1910/11 and celebrated with a dinner at the Royal Hotel, Attleborough. It was Mr William Gaymer, the president of the club (standing in the middle of the back row), who built up the cider firm from a one-man business to one employing four hundred people. Prominent in the Conservative Party, Mr Gaymer supported many local organizations and died in 1936.

Some London friends of Alfred 'Dear Boy' Smith, landlord of the Green Dragon at Wymondham, arrived in a Renault to visit him at the pub in 1914. 'Dear Boy' had moved to the town from London in 1890. Among locals in the picture are Ally Semmence, with a bowler at the back, and James Underwood, with a cap, holding the hand of his son Harry.

The committee of the Wymondham Ex-servicemen's Club soon after their Queen Street headquarters were officially opened by Charles Ayton in December 1922. With the demolition of the buildings in 1962, the club found a new home in Damgate, but now their premises are in Friarscroft Lane. Cyril Ayton, later the club's president, is second from the left in the back row.

Attleborough Salvation Army Band outside their hall in Chapel Road in 1932. Founded in 1883, the Attleborough Corps built up a strong membership but is now disbanded and the hall demolished. The bandmaster was William Hinchley, sitting on the right, while standing on the extreme right is 'Hallelujah' Brooks. James Woods is the man with the moustache on the left at the back.

Members of the Attleborough and Wymondham branches of Toc H, a Christian fellowship devoted to social service, parade their banners outside St Mary's Church, Attleborough, in the early 1950s. The Attleborough branch was founded in 1947 and Wymondham followed soon afterwards. Mr W.D. 'Bill' Gardiner, kneeling right, was instrumental in setting up the Attleborough branch.

Doctor George C. Gaynor sends down the first wood on the new Priory Park bowling green at Wymondham in 1959. The much loved GP had requested that a large proportion of a presentation fund set up to mark his retirement be used to provide the green for the enjoyment of elderly people. A prominent Conservative supporter, Doctor Gaynor had four spells as Chairman of Wymondham Urban District Council.

A church ladies group outside the rear of the old Attleborough Rectory in 1906, when the Revd Maxwell Webb was the rector. His son, Canon Ivo Webb, had the living for twenty-eight years from 1948 and, towards the end of that time, the Rectory was considered too big, so it was demolished. Holly Court old people's complex now stands on the site. The fourth lady from the right on the front row is Lillian Bowles (later Turner) and second from the right in the second row is Gertrude Bowles.

Earlier this century 'Granny' Woodbine, one of many characters at the time, lived in one of a row of cottages, which once stood just into Back Lane, off Pople Street, Wymondham. It was claimed that she was 'never seen without a cap, apron and plimsolls'.

Attleborough's Royal Mail van for the railway station service, soon after it was made at George Watling's Carriage Works in the town in 1903. The man holding the horse is Robert Everett, who lived in Chapel Road where the picture was taken, and the boy is believed to have been Bob Cowles.

Sam Marshall of Damgate, Wymondham, at Kett's Oak. Marshall, who sold hardware, was one of many itinerant dealers serving the area in the early years of the century. Before marching on Norwich in 1549, Robert Kett rallied his followers under an oak tree and legend has it that this was the one.

Fred 'Blacky' Elvin was a familiar figure in the Wymondham area, delivering milk by horse and cart up to the early 1950s. At one time he was employed by Albert Cross at Dykebeck, but later worked for Philip Fryer's Browick Dairy. The picture was taken on the Market Place and the shop in the background on the left was Fred Tillett's fish shop, which is now part of the Cross Keys pub.

Fire and Flood

Devastation caused by the fire at Parker's Supply Stores in Market Street, Wymondham on 9 September 1901. This was probably the biggest conflagration to hit the heart of the town since the great fire of 1615 and it broke out about 11.35p.m., soon bringing hundreds of people to the scene. The firefighters were hampered by a scant supply of water, and one flustered gentleman, eager to help salvage something, threw a dressing-table mirror out of the window and came downstairs with a feather-bed!

The New Buckenham Fire Brigade at Pump Court in the village soon after their formation in 1906. It was following a disastrous fire in that year (see page 110) that the villagers decided to form the brigade. The horse-drawn Merryweather engine was acquired and a crew recruited. Mr Gladwell, seated in the middle, was appointed captain. Their first call was to an elm tree, which caught fire when it was struck by lightning.

Attleborough firemen of yesteryear in celebratory mood. They are seen in a parade coming up Queen's Road towards the town centre.

The Wymondham Volunteer Fire Brigade, founded in 1882 under the superintendency of Mr E.B. Pomeroy, at a fire at Kimberley Hall. This was almost certainly the fire which occurred in August 1899 at the home of the Earl of Kimberley and severely gutted the servants' quarters. Dense clouds of smoke were visible from Wymondham.

The scene after one of the fires that broke out at S.D. Page & Sons' new brush factory at Wymondham in the 1890s. Rebuilding was soon undertaken, but another huge blaze destroyed the sawmills in 1924. The photograph was taken from White Horse Street looking up what is now Briton Way (then part of Lady's Lane).

The aftermath of the great fire in the Market Square at New Buckenham in February 1906. On the left are the gutted remains of the home of Arthur T. Clowes, a solicitor, and on the right all that remained of Mr W.N. Austin's grocery and drapery shop. Five brigades, including those from Attleborough and Wymondham, fought the blaze. The site of Mr Austin's shop is now used for car sales.

Surveying the wreckage after the fire at the Poynt House Saw Mills of Messrs George Semmence & Sons at Chapel Lane, Wymondham, in February 1914. The sawmills, three workshops and a large quantity of new machinery were destroyed.

Salvaging what was left of the International Stores at Attleborough after a serious fire broke out in the early hours of Sunday morning 4 June 1922. The town's fire brigade was handicapped by the inability to obtain water in the vicinity and water had to be pumped from a pond at Attleborough Hall. Incredibly, by Tuesday morning restoration had been completed, and the store was reopened with an entirely new stock!

Little was left of Arthur Howlett's Supply Stores at Bunwell after a big fire in January 1934. Owing to the nature of the stock, it was impossible to save the shop and the Wymondham fire brigade concentrated on saving the adjoining house. A strong wind was blowing, but luckily away from the house! The stores were rebuilt by the following year.

All hands to the pumps! This was the last occasion Wymondham's 22-man manual pump, dating from 1882, was used. 'Rhubarb' Underwood's fair lorry and trailer had caught fire on the Spooner Row side of the Suton level crossing. Behind can be seen Semmence's Renault 24 horsepower breakdown truck, which was used for towing the fire appliance.

A sad Harold Carter surveys the wreckage after the famous North Mill at Wymondham had been destroyed by fire on Friday 17 February 1950. The water supply to the town was seriously affected by the operations to fight the blaze, which it was believed started in the mill's engine-room. Two appliances from Wymondham, two from Attleborough and one from Norwich attended the fire.

The Wymondham Fire Brigade with their new Dennis 'Ace' engine at the time it was purchased for them by the Urban District Council in 1935. It was the town's first motorized fire appliance and was a self-propelled pump with a capacity of 350–450 gallons per minute. The man in the driving seat is Frank Elkins, the brigade's chief officer between 1941 and 1948.

The Tiffey Bridge at Station Road, Wymondham, after seven inches of rain fell on Monday 26 August 1912. It was here that Mr Laycock, a local pork butcher, had his pony and cart carrying pigs washed away by the flood.

Pictures like this one of 'the houses of Hubbard and Nicholls', at Damgate Bridge in Wymondham, appeared in many national dailies in that August of 1912. The occupants had barely time to leave their homes before they were washed away.

The scene at the Bannister Bridge in Attleborough during the great flood of 1912. It was here that a local carter took advantage of the horrific conditions by ferrying pedestrians across the water at a 'penny return'.

SECTION TWELVE

Wartime

Boer War Celebrations at Wymondham. With flags draped across the Market Place and banners proclaiming 'Welcome Home' and 'Thankful Hearts', the town celebrated the return of members of the F (Wymondham) Company of the 4th Volunteer Battalion, Norfolk Regiment, from South Africa in May 1901. People flocked to the station to shake the hands of the soldiers and there was a torchlight procession, headed by a band, round the town. Among those who had served with distinction were Lieutenant B. Maurice Hughes, a popular local doctor, and Charles Cranness, who joined the Company as a 14-year-old bugler. More festivities followed news of the Boer surrender in May 1902.

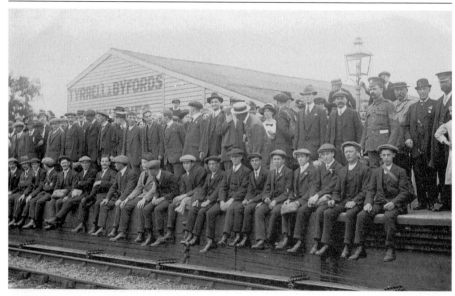

Volunteers on Attleborough station platform waiting to go to Norwich to enlist in August 1914 at the start of the First World War. With the outbreak of hostilities, patriotic men from the Attleborough and Wymondham district flocked to serve their country, mainly in Lord Kitchener's New Army. A recruiting office in Attleborough was set up in Captain John Kennedy's house at Attleborough Lodge. In the photograph, the man in uniform by the lamppost is Sergeant Dickerson.

An Essex Regiment 'supply train' in London Road, Attleborough, in late 1914.

Men of the 4th Service Battalion of the Essex Regiment in the yard of the Windmill public house at Wymondham in late 1914. The battalion arrived in November and several were billeted along Norwich Road. They set up stores in Church Street, and many were sorry to leave the town at the end of January 1915.

The Town Hall, which housed Attleborough's Auxiliary Red Cross Hospital. Handed over by its directors in August 1914, the building saw service until November 1917, by which time the much bigger Wayland Infirmary was in use.

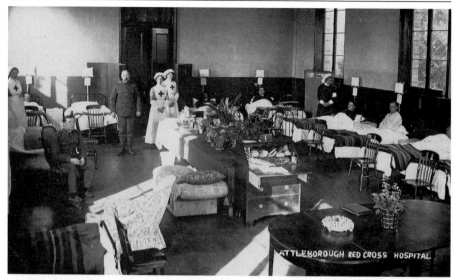

The inside of Attleborough's neat Red Cross Hospital. Initially, it was fitted with sixteen beds, but this was later increased to twenty-three. The commandant was Mrs J.H. Kennedy. The Red Cross Hospital treated 656 patients, while the Wayland Infirmary, requisitioned as a military hospital in April 1917, with 100 beds, cared for 997 patients between then and April 1919.

Nurses and patients at the Red Cross Hospital at Abbotsford in Vicar Street, Wymondham. In November 1914 the Vicarage Room, which stood on the site of the present Abbey Hall, was taken over as the hospital, but because of the inadequate number of beds, Captain and Mrs H.L. Cautley offered the use of part of their Abbotsford home. The commandant from 1914 until her untimely death in 1918 was Mrs Rose Martin-Jones, the vicar's wife, who sits in the front row between her husband and Dr Penn Young, the medical officer in charge.

A parade in Church Street, Attleborough, with no disrupting traffic! Many regiments passed through Norfolk during the conflict and this is the 4th Northamptonshire Regiment. John Butler's once popular store can be seen behind the lamppost.

'Feed the Guns' Week at Wymondham in November 1918. This was held to raise funds for the war effort just as the armistice was being signed. As part of the proceedings, six mules drew an 18 pounder field gun, which had seen service in France, from the station to the Market Place.

Peace celebrations at Wymondham on 19 July 1919. Events included a united church service, rural sports and this dinner for discharged men. The meal was served in the 'new' Drill Hall in Pople Street by the Welcome Home Committee.

The scene at Attleborough on Sunday 27 June 1920 just after the Earl of Albemarle had unveiled the war memorial. The Revd P.M. Hoyle, Primitive Methodist minister, is seen giving a short address. Wymondham's war memorial was similarly unveiled and dedicated on a Sunday in July 1921.

Sandbags protect Wymondham Police Station, then situated in the Bridewell, soon after the outbreak of the Second World War in 1939. District Superintendent S.H. Bushell is on the left and Constable Robert 'Speed Cop' White is third from the left.

One of many pillboxes erected in the area early in the war. The picture of this one at Attleborough, which hides the town's Crimean war memorial, was taken in 1944 by an American serviceman, who was based at Old Buckenham with the 453rd Bomb Group.

Attleborough's special constables in the gardens of the Royal Hotel during the war. In the middle of the front row is District Superintendent S.H. Bushell and among the group are several well-known local businessmen. Among them are Robert McKelvie (back row, fourth left), Clarence Matthews (second row, second left) and Geoffrey Cooke (the man in civvies).

Attleborough's ARP Ambulance Station personnel in 1941–2. The picture was taken in the yard behind the Angel Hotel, where there used to be a shed which housed the cars and ambulances. Among the ladies are Doris Francis (back row, first left), Bertha Taylor (later Riches, front row, first left) and Joyce Westley (front row, right). One incident attended was when a plane came down and hit Hargham Church.

The devastation caused in the bottling department at Gaymer's after a lone German plane dropped high explosive and oil bombs during the morning of 30 December 1940. The raider's machine-guns were continually firing and there were seven casualties. Among those injured were Robert Doughty and Cyril 'Sticky' Lloyd, whose nickname derived from his job in the sugar room.

Wymondham firemen, preparing for any emergency, at a training session at Wymondham Laundry in 1942. The laundry building particularly lent itself to ladder drills. Behind, on the left, is an Austin Towing Vehicle and, on the right, the Dennis 'Ace' engine. Reg Cullum, later to become Officer-in-Charge, is on the extreme right. During the war, there were static water tanks at White Horse Street and Town Green.

The Royal Observer Corps on a march past in Wymondham's Market Street in the early 1940s. Leading the way are Arthur Ogden, who is saluting, and Dick Young. Following behind the corps are ARP wardens.

Inspection of a parade on the Market Hill at Wymondham during the Wymondham Forehoe and Henstead War Weapons Week in April 1941. The firemen being inspected by Field Marshall Lord Ironside are from the right, Arthur Banham, Herbert Ringer, Ben Dove and George Ayers. On the left is Reggie Bird, the brigade's Officer-in-Charge.

Old Buckenham, home to the 453rd Bomb Group pictured here, was just one of many bases occupied by the United States Army Eighth Air Force from 1942 onwards. Others included those at Deopham Green, Hethel and Tibenham. The picture shows briefing rooms, the aircrew mess and, at the back, the perimeter track. Actor James Stewart served at Old Buckenham.

Members of the Wymondham Fire Service with American allies in 1943. The picture was probably taken at the Hethel base, home to the 320th Bomb Group and later the 389th. The fire service personnel are (left to right), William Howlett, Reggie Long and Barbara Long.

A typical scene at the American Army Air Force Hospital at Morley in the latter years of the war. The hospital was built on the site of the Mid-Norfolk Golf Club course and was handed to the Americans in September 1943, with the 231st Station Hospital moving in the next year. In the months following D-Day to the end of 1944, eight train-loads of casualties, totalling 2,099 patients, arrived at the hospital via Wymondham railway station. The hospital closed in June 1945 and became for a time a transit camp for the Royal Norfolk Regiment. Teacher training colleges were housed in the buildings from 1947 until 1950, when it became the home of Wymondham College.

The Anglo-American Services' Club in Town Green at Wymondham. The club for allied servicemen was situated in the former Picture House and was run by the Church Army. It was declared open by Lord Walsingham on 15 March 1943.

A 'Candy Parade' at Alf Harvey's fish and chip shop in Damgate, Wymondham, in December 1943. Playing Father Christmas, United States Air Force personnel hand out sweets, biscuits and other goodies to over three hundred children from the Infant and Junior Schools. Many special relationships developed between 'Yanks' and 'Brits' in those austere times, and many survived long after hostilities ceased.

Acknowledgements

The author is grateful to the following people, who generously loaned pictures for this book:

Mrs B. Barrett • R. Bartram • R. Bentley • M. Blazey • Revd E. Buck
F. Bushell • A. Cardy • Mrs D. Codd • A. Cross • Eastern Counties Newspapers
Mrs M. Edwards • Mrs F. Fields • E.J. Fowler • W. Gaymer & Son Ltd
K. Gee • G. Gosling • Gressenhall Rural Life Museum
Hamilton Acorn Ltd (Julian Massie) • B. Hardyman • Mrs G. Harvey
Mrs A. Hoare • B. Hill • M. Johnson • G. Mabbutt • R. Myhill
Old Buckenham Cricket Club • F. Parsons • B. Plunkett • C.A. Proctor
P. Ramm • B. Self • H. Semmence & Co. • A. Smith • P. Smith • D. Standley
P. Standley • Mrs E. Suggitt • J. Tann • C.R. Temple • Mrs C. Tofts
Mrs M. Townsend • W. Tunaley • P. Wade • M. Wadesley • R. West
P. Wharton • T. Wood • Wymondham Town Archives (Janet Smith)

Thanks are also due to the many people who have offered snippets of information, in particular Claude Edwards, Bill Gardiner, George Mabbutt and Lily Wire, together with Janet Smith of the Wymondham Town Archives, and the Norwich Local Studies Library.

Special thanks to Terry Burchell for his photographic work, Richard Barham for reading the text, my daughter Joanne for word-processor duties and my wife Wendy for bearing with me.